EDVARD MUNCH

PER AMANN

EDVARD MUNCH

Artline Editions

Translated by Jennifer Barnes

English Language Rights: Artlines UK Ltd, **2** Castle Street,
Thornbury, Bristol. Avon, England
Printed in West Germany – Imprimé en Allemagne
ISBN 1 871487 02 1

CONTENTS

I have spent my whole life half in a dream and half in reality. Men have understood this and have preyed on my defenceless body with their tigers' teeth, while my soul was voyaging elsewhere.

E. Munch

In 1892, an artistic battle was fought out in Berlin that was to have far-reaching consequences. The Norwegian painter Edvard Munch had been invited to a big exhibition, but no-one had suspected the extraordinary nature of the man. Munch travelled to Berlin with 55 paintings and precipitated an immense uproar in the whole world of representational art. The academics at the Berlin Artists' Union forced the closure of the exhibition and declared Munch deranged. The rising faction for the regeneration of art condemmed this move, and formed an opposition party, with Max Liebermann at its head. This counter-movement was the inspiration for the creative work of the Berlin Secession, and it was Munch, coming from a completely different world, who was the indirect impetus behind it.

It fell to Edvard Munch to have an effect on younger generations of artists comparable to Vincent van Gogh's. Like him, he was self-reliant and able to state what he believed with considerable force. He was born on December 12th, 1863, in Loten, Hedmark, in Norway. His father was a morose man, a doctor in the poor quarter of Oslo, and his pitiful income barely sufficed to feed the seven members of his family. Thus, from the first stirrings of his awareness, Edvard was hemmed in by poverty and privation. When he was only five years old, the sensitive boy watched his mother die from consumption. A few years later, his sister Sophie suffered the same fate, and another sister died of mental derangement. It is all too easy to understand that these events made a lasting and painful impression on the boy's spiritual development. He was possessed by a nameless fear that he too would be overtaken by a similar fate, and this fear held him in thrall for half his life. After his mother's death, her younger sister ran the household in her place, and was certainly a formative influence on the life of the boy Edvard, who had been awakened so early and so rudely to the grim realities of life. She evidently realised that fear loses its grip once it finds expression in words or pictures, for she insisted that the growing boy should take up painting and drawing, and thus set him on the right path. Nevertheless, those early experiences of death never faded from Munch's consciousness. Even 26 years later, when he was recording his "Memories of Childhood" in his drawings, his distress had not waned. Writing almost as an observer, he noted on the back of them his original impressions, still fresh in his mind: "At the bottom end of the big double bed, they sat close together on two little children's chairs; the tall figure of a woman stood to one side, dark and imposing against the window. She said that she would leave them – and asked whether they would be unhappy, if she were no longer there – and they had to promise her to stay close to Jesus, and then they would see each other again in heaven.

They did not really understand it all – but they found it terribly sad, and then they both wept – wept bitterly –."

For Edvard Munch, his awakening to conscious life was an experience of the most profound inner pain. In an attempt to come to terms with this his inheritance of suffering, he made it the perception and so the root of his creative achievement. His art contains nothing that is ordinary or traditional in style; it is all an expression of a deeper meaning. Since the conservative artists of the Berlin Academy were not privy to his personal history, they were incapable of understanding the paintings of the 29-year-old Munch, paintings which must indeed have seemed to them to alienate the eye and flout accepted principles. Those among the younger artists who were seeking an alternative, were startled into action by the drastic and sometimes uncompromising manner in which Munch did not hesitate to make emotion the subject of his paintings.

Throughout his life, Munch had been a keen draughtsman. In 1880 he decided, with his father's agreement, to abandon his engineering studies and to become a painter. He took lessons from Christian Krohg in Oslo, among others, and practised his art in life studies, portraits, and genre painting. In 1885, he, too, was seduced by the powerful attraction of Paris as an artistic centre. Like every aspiring artist, he was seeking self-assertion and recognition. His first visit only lasted for three weeks, it is true, and yet there can be no doubt that he was impelled to new efforts by the journey, by the city itself, and by the new impressions that crowded in on him. In 1889, he went to Paris for the second time, this time not as a visiting observer but as a student. He enrolled with Léon Bonnat and studied the French Impressionists. He sympathised with the subjects that had moved them, and this sympathy made new demands on his own work. He wrote in his diary: "No more interiors should be painted, no people reading, no women knitting. They should be living human beings, who breathe and feel, suffer and love. – I should like to produce a whole series of such pictures".

In the ensuing years the 'Frieze of Life' first took shape, in a version that was more an expression of intent, being preliminary sketches rather than completed work. The theme was so powerfully conceived that it occupied him for twenty years and called for constant reworkings.

Till 1892, Munch remained in France, supported by government grants, and frequently breaking off to travel to his homeland in the north. He was actively employed in working for publishers and newspapers, and submitted his pictures to reputable exhibitions. In the autumn of 1892 the "Munch affair" blew up in Berlin, and overnight he became a force to be reckoned with throughout the German-speaking world. In spite of the resulting outcry, he put down roots in Berlin, and, during the subsequent years, it was there that he worked almost exclusively. He held his own views on Germany and its art: "However badly art in general is served in Germany, I must say one thing: it has the advantage of bringing out individual artists who far outrank all others and are in a class of their own – for example, Böcklin, who in my opinion stands head and shoulders above almost all our contemporary painters, Max Klinger, Thoma, Wagner in music, Nietzsche in philosophy. Art in France is superior to art in Germany, but can boast no one artist greater than those I have mentioned." (Excerpt from a letter to J. Rode in Copenhagen).

Within a diffuse circle of artists and writers, Munch often encountered his fellow-countryman August Strindberg and the Polish poet inspired by Nietzsche, Stanislaw Przybyszewski, and indulged in lively exchanges of views with them. In particular, he was deeply affected by the Symbolist and Expressionist idiom of the latter. He wanted to represent in a pictorial form what Przybyszewski had expressed in words, an all-embracing cycle of human life. Thus were born, in Berlin between 1893 and 1895, those pictures which contained the kernel of Munch's expressionist world and which were the foundation of his fame: "The Voice", "Madonna", "Vampire", "Melancholy", and "The scream", to name but a few. They were all the first manifestations of themes which were to obsess him throughout his life and which he recreated, often scarcely altered, or translated into other techniques. Later, Munch himself was to give an account of the evolution of one of these trail-blazing new paintings: "My first sight of the sick child made an impression on me that evaporated as I worked – the picture that appeared on the canvas was good, but it was not the same. – I painted it again, several times, in the course of a year – scratched it out, let the colours blend into each other – and constantly tried to recapture my first impression: the transparently pale skin, the trembling mouth, the shaking hands. I had painted the chair with the glass on it in too much detail: it distracted attention from the head – when I looked at the painting, all I could see was the glass and its background. Should I get rid of it completely? No, it helped to contour the head more clearly and to bring it into focus. I scratched the background half out and left all the essential elements as they were. One saw the head and the glass.Then I discovered that my own eyelashes had contributed to the impression the picture made, and so I indicated them as shadows over the painting. Somehow, the head became the picture – Wavy lines took shape in the painting – on the periphery – with the head at the centre. Later, I was to make frequent use of these wavy lines. Finally I gave up in exhaustion. To a great extent, I had realised my original impression: the trembling mouth, the transparent skin, the tired eyes. However, the colour was still not right; it was too pale and too grey, and as a result the whole effect was heavy as lead. In the years 1895 and 1906 I returned to working on this painting, and gave it more of the strong colour I had been aiming for. I painted three versions. – They are all different, and in its own way each contributes to the feelings aroused in me by my first encounter with the model. – With "The Sick Child" I was setting out in new directions: it became a breakthrough in my art. Most of my later pictures derive from this painting. No painting had aroused as much anger in Norway as this one. When I entered the room where it was hanging on the opening day of the exhibition, there was a crowd of people milling round the picture; you could hear screams of horror and laughter".

In the last years of the century, Munch was on the one hand working away feverishly, on the other constantly on the move, driven between France, Italy, Germany, and Scandinavia. He bought a small house in Asgardstrand, which was henceforward to serve as a refuge and summer holiday home. It was not only his profession as a painter and the many exhibitions of his paintings that disrupted his life; rather it was the range of his experiences, his childhood, his father's death, all combined to seethe and tunnel within him. The constant alternation between clinical depression and excited elation preyed on his strength, until excessive exhaustion finally forced him to enter a sanatorium for a cure. However, he could not be prevented from working relentlessly on his "Frieze of Life".

In 1902, he embarked on a prolonged stay in Berlin. Although Munch was subjected by the newspaper critics to misunderstanding and rejection, he was establishing a reputation for himself, the band of his adherents and patrons was growing larger, and as a result he was getting well paid commissions. He would spend the summer months partly in the homely surroundings of Asgardstrand, in the simplicity of his much-loved wooden house, and then, after extensive travel, he would be drawn back to the allure of the great city. He was fascinated by the richness of social intercourse and the study of other walks of life, as a contrast to the northern solitudes, whose inhabitants are absorbed into the overweening life of nature itself. A phenomenon that Munch once put into words: "I feel the clamour of nature." He painted many portraits and so came to know respected figures on the Berlin scene. In 1906, Max Reinhardt, then on the threshold of his career, was looking for a suitable artist to undertake the decor for a new production of Ibsen's "Ghosts", and settled on his new acquaintance, Munch, who at once entered into the spirit of the play. The production enjoyed huge success, and Reinhardt declared that he had never been so stimulated by an artist as he was by Munch. Arthur Kahane, Reinhardt's dramaturge, has left an account of that time: "And so Edvard Munch was daily in the Deutsches Theater and lived among us, painting by day and drinking by night, and working alternately on the "Ghosts" paintings and on his own cycle. Sometimes he would sit motionless for long, long periods, in complete silence... And then some small thing would break the spell and he would wake up, bright and full of laughter: the artless, joyous laughter of children. His nature was invariably friendly, and yet somehow buttoned up, with a nordic reserve, close and impenetrable. To us he remained a stranger, an enigma. He had something of a child, of a wild thing, primaeval as an animal, innocent as Parsifal."

This period of creativity confirmed his reputation and fame, but had an adverse effect on his health. In 1908 Jens Thiis, director of the Nasjonalgalleriet in Oslo, paid him the tribute of purchasing several of his pictures for the museum. But the dying year found him in Dr. Daniel Jacobson's clinic in Copenhagen, at the mercy of yet another nervous breakdown. Since 1902, after the dramatic break-up of his relationship with Tulla Larson, who had been close to him and had exerted a great influence on his life, his nerves had been in shreds and he seemed incurable. An ever-increasing consumption of alcohol caused a visible deterioration in his condition, until a complete psychiatric and physical collapse was inevitable. During the year he spent at the sanatorium he achieved a measure of internal peace, with the help of his understanding doctor. He wrote the legend "Alpha and Omega", that tells of a woman's deceit, and illustrated it with lithographs. He wrote it, in fact, as a sort of liberation within his inner conflicts, and through it was released from the coils of the powers of darkness.

In 1909 he returned to Norway and took part in the competition for the decoration of the Aula of the new Oslo University. At 45, after years of restless wanderings abroad, he sought the peace of his homeland, and accordingly settled in the idyllic countryside at Kragerö on Oslo Fjord. Hoping for recognition in his own country, he devoted himself to his studies and to sketches for the University Aula. The competition was judged, the jury rejected the other candidates but was reluctant to recognise Munch as the winner, suggesting that there should be a second competition between Munch and his only serious rival, Emanuel Vigeland, and that this time it should include designs for the Aula as a whole. The elaboration of the sketches for it was a deciding factor in the new phase of Munch's painting. The themes were no longer inspired by the spiritual world of the "Frieze of Life"; he had broken free from the clutches of the terrible nervous breakdowns. The central picture of this, the most monumental project he ever undertook, was a sun, reigning supreme, in a framework of 4.5 x 7.8 metres. The surrounding paintings were conceived so that their content was also related to this central sun, thus extending its influence beyond the confines of its actual measurements. Munch wrote of his sketches, of which there were well over a hundred: "My intention was that the designs should form an independent and self-sufficient world of ideas, and that its visual expression should be both typically Norwegian and at the same time universally human".

Meanwhile, in 1911 the jury was still undecided. True, Vigeland's design was to be rejected, but Jens Thiis was, as ever, the only judge to give Munch's work his unqualified approval. The jury haggled over compromises, agreed in 1912 that the paintings should be provisionally installed, but instructed Munch to continue working on them.

As late as March 1914, the purchase of the designs was deemed desirable and in 1916, the work was finally ceremonially unveiled. "The Frieze of Life is an intimate representation of the joys and sorrows of man as an individual, while the University designs portray the great, eternal strengths." Thus Munch describes this part of his oeuvre.

In his home country, there was never any question but that his standing would be recognised by the Norwegians themselves. Even if their nordic reserve prevented them from overt approval, as the years went by he received countless accolades and prestigious commissions. And yet few enough of his contemporaries were blessed with any real understanding of his art. A valid interpretation of the thought behind the paintings demanded an explanation of every last detail. Even in pictures of everyday scenes, like "Woodcutter", "Galloping Horse", or "Workers in the Snow", Munch was looking beyond the foreground. His pictures made heavy demands on the viewer, who had been long accustomed to having beauty as the primary concern of any painting.

In 1916 Munch bought the estate of Ekely, just outside Oslo. Here he was able to set up a large studio and gradually to assemble his Frieze of Life around him. Some pictures were reworked, others started afresh, with the aim of giving full expression to his ideas. He himself explained what he hoped to achieve with his Frieze: "It is seen as a series of related paintings, which combine to form a picture of life. Throughout the whole frieze runs the shore line, curving away into the distance, behind which surges the evermoving sea; under the treetops life breathes in all its richness, with all its sorrows and all its joys. The frieze is perceived as a poem of life, of love, and of death. The design of the largest painting – 'Man and woman in a wood' – perhaps deviates a little from the pattern of the other pictures, but nonetheless it is a necessary part of the whole; it forms the clasp that fastens the belt. This picture of two naked people 'Man and woman in a wood', with the town appearing in the distance, is a portrayal of life and death: the wood, which sucks life from the dead, the town that grows up behind the treetops; this is the picture of the strong and all-powerful forces of life."

Munch's later work belongs for the most part to a second cycle, the "Worker paintings". He was destined always to feel himself an outsider, excluded from bourgeois society. In the socially inferior working classes, he saw men who were on his own level, disadvantaged as he was. "The sense I had since childhood of being the victim of a deadly injustice was the foundation for the activist tendencies in my work," he wrote, in his autobiographical notes.

He had always liked to sketch farmers, weavers, and working men in general. Like van Gogh, such subjects were close to his heart. From 1910 onwards, he identified himself ever more closely with this motif, and from 1920, he devoted himself almost exclusively to the representation of work and workers. He felt the workers' privations as his own, and incorporated his unfulfilled dreams of greater equality in life into his paintings of them. Above his picture "Workers on the way home" he wrote: "Do you know who it is walking here? It is me. The bourgeois mob has tried to force me, too, to my knees." And of his work in his own country, he wrote: "As long as I have been painting in this country, I have had to fight with clenched fist for every last toe-hold for my art. I have also put a man with a clenched fist as the central figure in my big worker painting."

In spite of all the social criticism inherent in his pictures, Munch was devoid of politcal ambition. The aims of the workers' movement and their social circumstances were overlaid with his own subjective experiences, and he felt their justification. He was not a political animal as such; he was a realist rather than an idealist, and yet he did not depict reality itself, but the reality of an event, a motive. He wanted to capture not the fact, but its cause. "I do not paint what I see but what I have seen." The shy, retiring, solitary painter did not combat grievances with traditional weapons; instead he incorporated them into the background of his canvases, expressed the essence of them, and hoped that this message would be understood. His wrath was directed against the whole of the bourgeoisie. Even the shape of his pictures was a challenge to salon painting; as he put it: "Small pictures with large frames represent bourgeois art, art that is intended for the drawing-room. It is art for art-dealers, a product of the French revolution. Now is the time of the workers. Surely art should once again become the property of all men, and return to its rightful place in public buildings and on great walls?" – "Modern architecture consists of smooth surfaces and spaces – small pictures are no longer necessary. – But large areas need life and colour . . . Should we not revert to wall paintings as they did in the renaissance? Then art will once again become the property of the people; works of art will belong to us all –."

One commission that was true to this spirit was the "Freia project". As a result of a commercial success, the chocolate factory Freia needed to record its history by redecorating its canteens in a modern and artistic style. One large and two smaller rooms were planned, but only the large one was actually completed. Munch was excited by the prospect of attempting to incorporate some of his worker themes into a new frieze, a "Workers frieze". The frieze was to remind workers of their various freedoms, and so he began with a painting he had already conceived, "Workers leave the Factory". Another picture in the six-part frieze is called "The Mechanic meets his daughter", the same subject as the work he had produced in 1908 called "Worker and

Child", with slight alterations, including the factory in the background. Other paintings show a walk through the town, a trip into the country: not work, but the end of work, free time; a concept that was at that time foreign to everyday language. Again and again, he would revitalise earlier paintings by reworking them or setting them in new contexts, a process which was most certainly not caused by lack of imagination, but by the fact that these pictures were not decorations. They were the precise elaboration of his own world of ideas, the expression of his being, and so they were to remain valid and contemporary. His notes give us an indication why Munch preferred to execute his paintings in groups: "How I came to murals and friezes. – In my art, I have attempted to clarify life and the meaning it holds for me. I also wanted to help others to explain life to themselves. I have always worked best when surrounded by my own pictures. – I felt that the content of the pictures was interrelated. – When I put them together, they suddenly acquired a resonance which was lacking when they were alone. – In the same way, it was impossible to exhibit them together with other pictures. – So that is why I grouped them together as a frieze."

In Ekely, he surrounded himself with those of his previous canvases that were essential to his work and dear to his heart. No matter whether they were sketches or illustrations, he was reluctant to part from anything, for any scene, once captured, could serve later as a source of inspiration. He thus looked on most of his woodcuts and etchings, his water colours and even oil paintings as preliminary studies for his great monumental projects. In the late twenties, Munch decided to have a winter studio added at Ekely, and his observations of the building work involved were the inspiration for countless sketches. These, along with many he had made of roadworks in the city streets, were to figure in the designs for the decoration of the new town hall in Oslo. However, problems of community politics and the enforced demolition of several buildings delayed completion of his plans. When the foundation stone finally came to be laid in 1931, Munch's health no longer permitted him to devote himself to the colossal undertaking of the complete repainting of the new building. Trouble with his eyes forced him to curtail his activities, and it was at this period that he produced many lithographs and woodcuts, along with graphic versions of earlier sections of the Frieze of Life.

One element that runs like a thread throughout Munch's whole life and work is the self-portraits. They can be traced through various periods, although it is the final years that are particularly impressive. Increasingly, Munch withdrew into his studio and cut himself off from the outside world. Political events, war, his illness, all combined to make him even shyer towards the public and to encourage solitude. These remarks from a visitor in 1937 give us an idea of his appearance: "Upstairs, Munch stood in the doorway, motionless, like a candle, with his head lifted, like a blind man. His face was thin, his features stamped with an old man's beauty. His eyes were grey-blue, rather weary; a line of self-denial played around his compressed lips. His ears were large and well-shaped. Fine, silky hair fell over the reddish forehead."

His self portraits "Night Wanderer", (1939), "At the Window" and "Between the Clock and the Bed" (1940) reflect the constant narrowing of the world that framed his life. His work, on the other hand, won ever wider acclaim. As unflinchingly as he persisted with his own work, in spite of reduced circumstances, so the public persisted with its arrangements for exhibitions. The painter and graphic artist Edvard Munch is a recognised representative of modern Norwegian art. It is true that his pictures in Germany, along with those of the other Expressionists, did not escape confiscation as "Degenerate art", but by the same token his standing in Scandinavia was enhanced.

A few days after his eightieth birthday, when honours were heaped upon him, he witnessed the terrible explosion at an ammunitions dump in Oslo harbour. Terrified, the old man took refuge in the cellars of his house and caught a severe chill; he never recovered from its effects and on January 23rd., 1944 he died peacefully in Ekely. The town of Oslo inherited from Munch, inexhaustible worker that he was, the bequest of about 1000 oil paintings, 15 000 prints, and 4 400 water colours and drawings.

He was blessed with the tragic gift of experiencing in his inmost soul whatever was happening around him, and with the strength not to be overcome by the burden this imposed: "I would not be without suffering; I owe so much in my art to suffering."

Oskar Kokoschka sums up Munch's oeuvre in the following terms: "Edvard Munch had the ability, through the unusual perception of his eye, to diagnose the terror of cosmic fear in apparently opportunistic progress."

ILLUSTRATIONS

Edvard 95

Plate I

The day after. 1894
Nasjonalgalleriet, Oslo

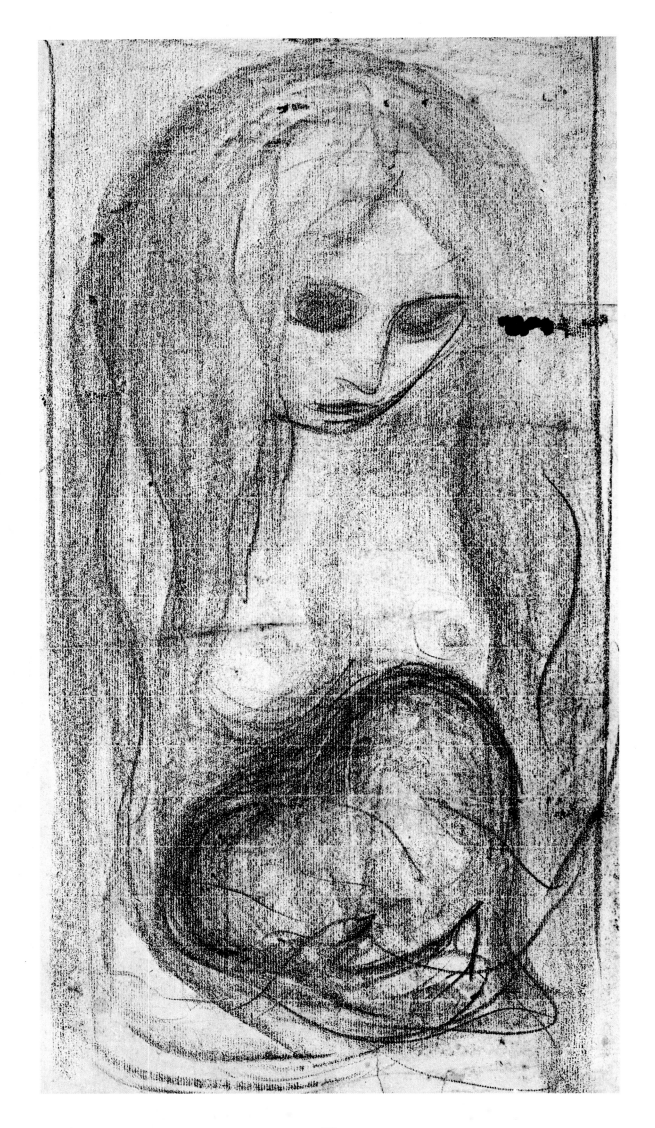

Plate II

The dance of life. 1899–1900
Nasjonalgalleriet, Oslo

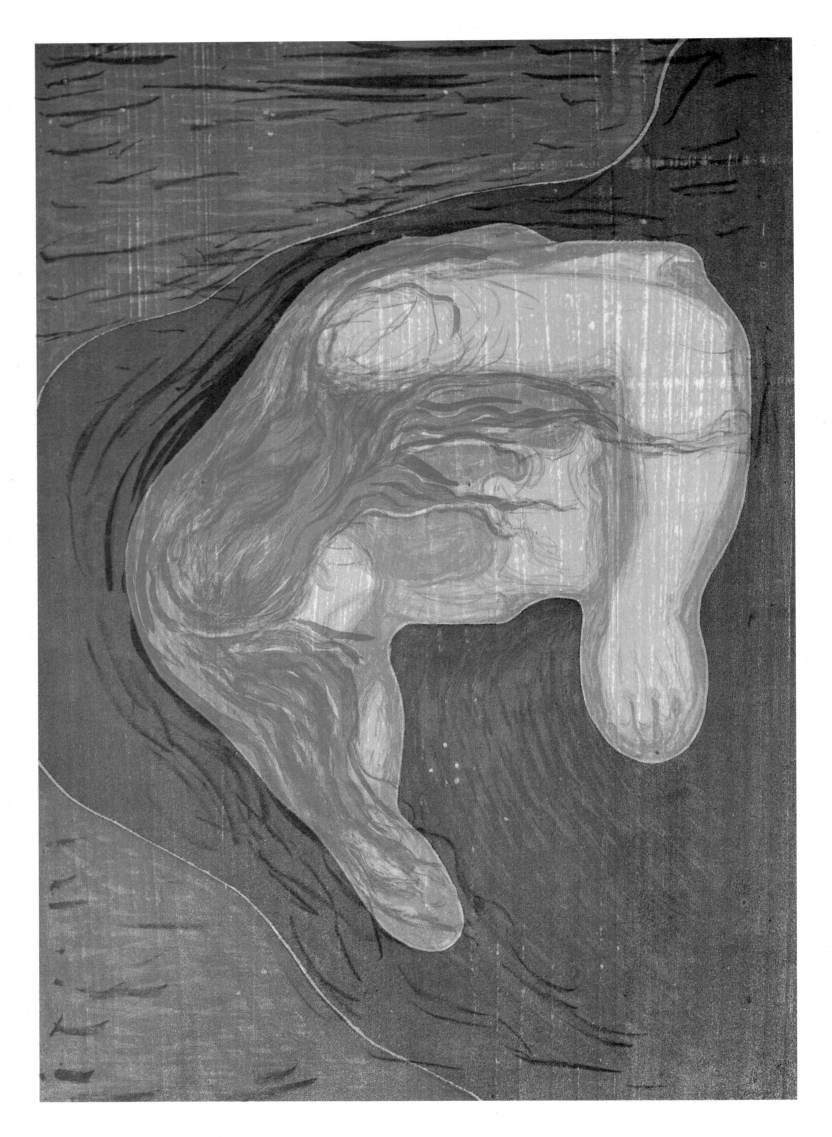

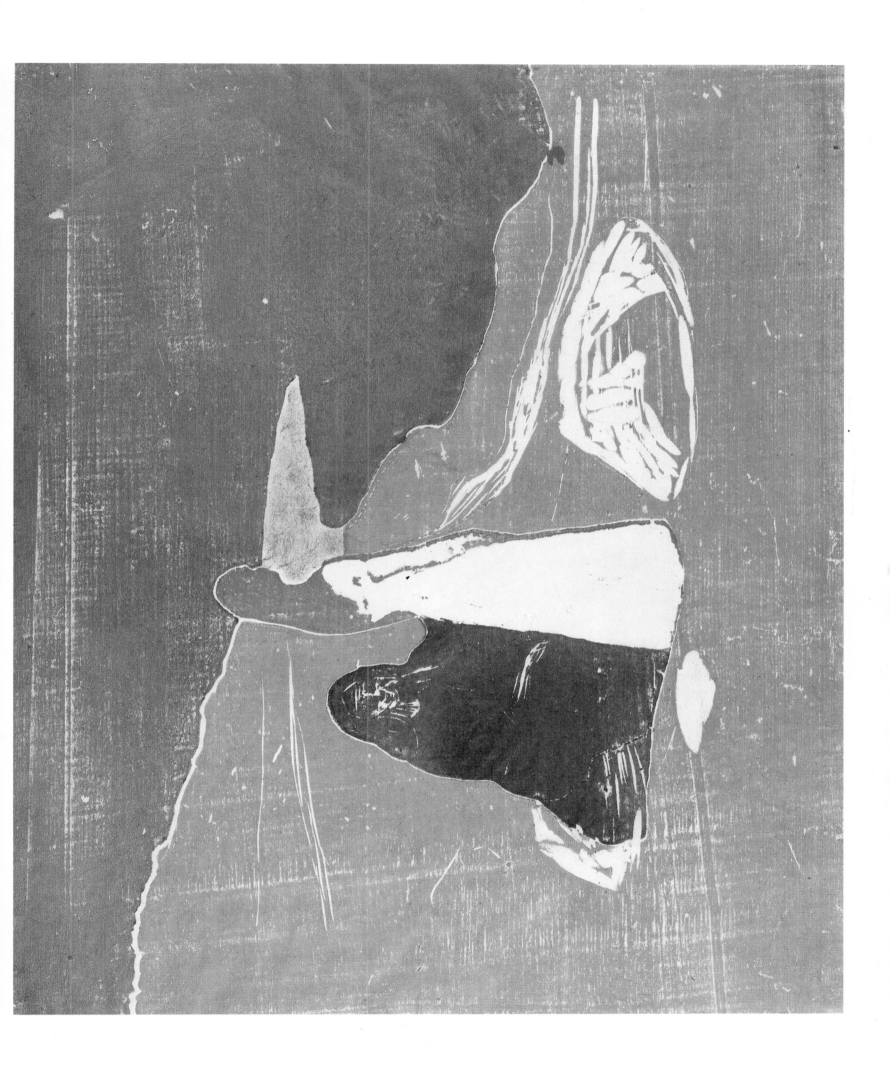

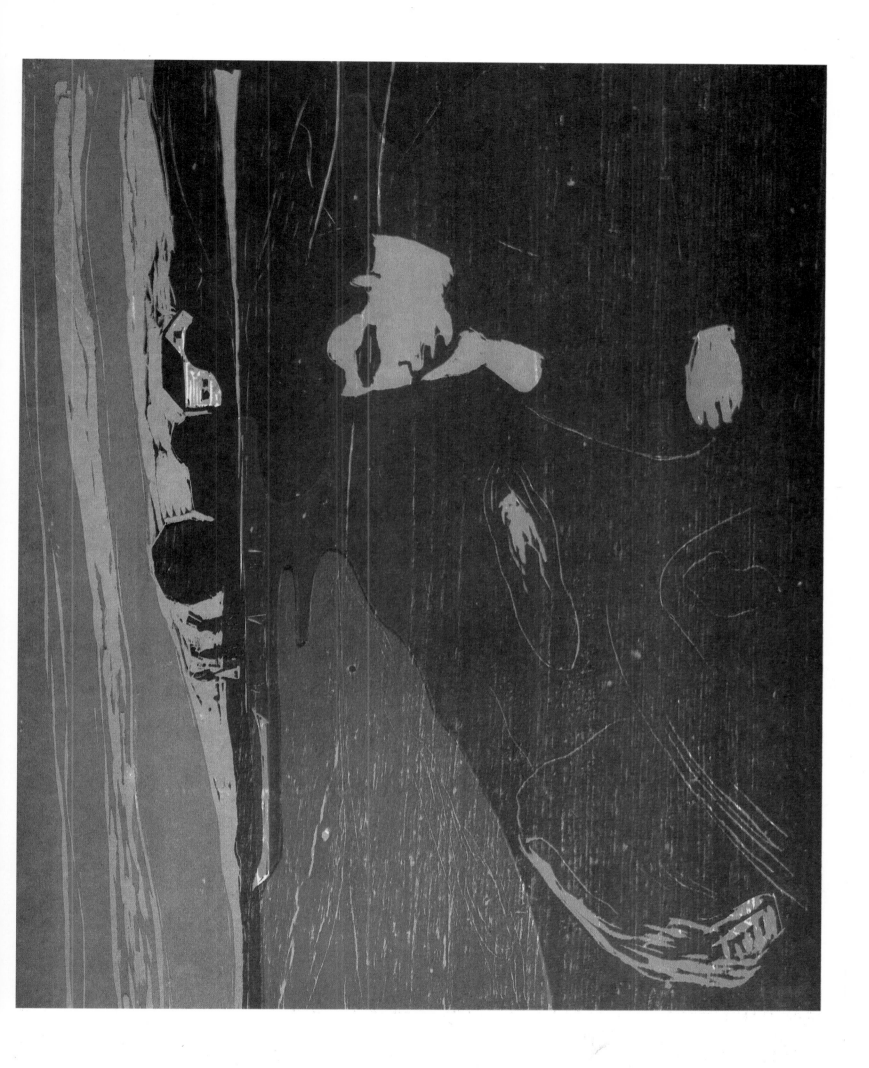

Plate III

Woman with red hair. 1898–1902
Munch-Museet, Oslo

Plate IV

Winter night. Around 1900
Kunsthaus Zürich

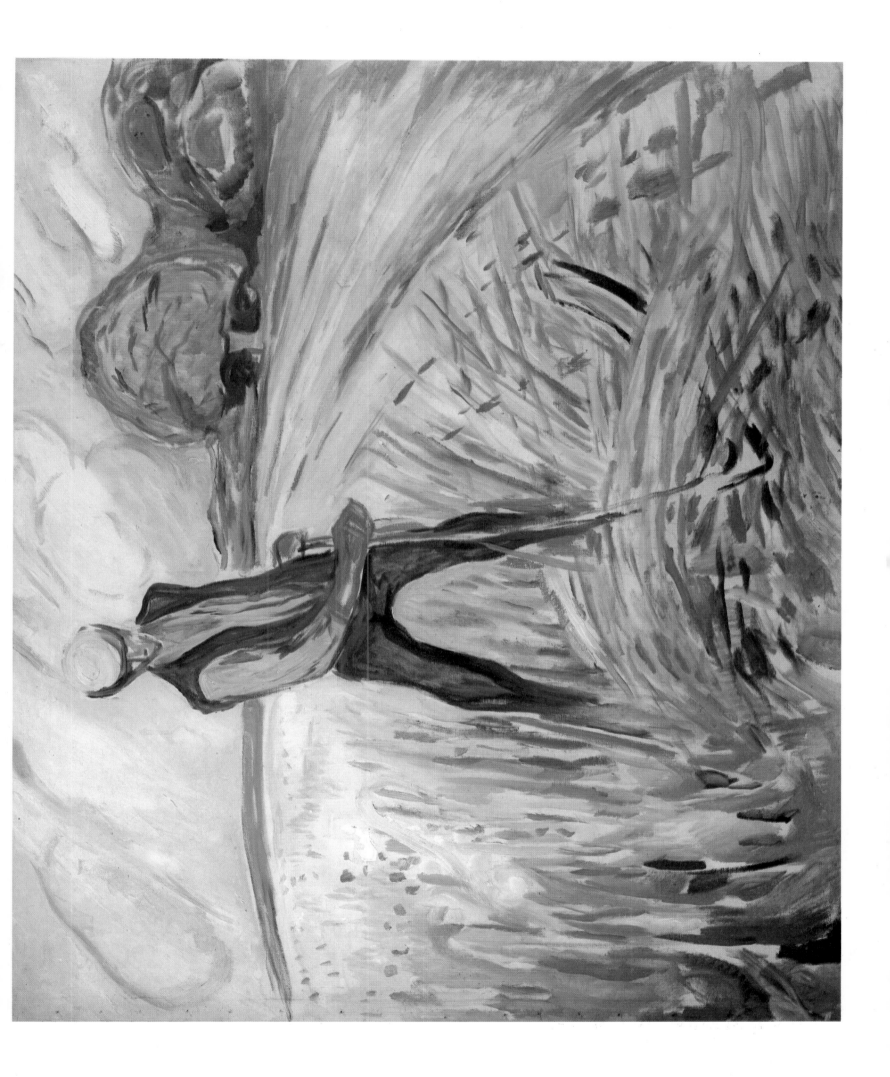

52

Plate V

Horses ploughing. 1919
Nasjonalgalleriet, Oslo

Plate VI

Three girls on the bridge. 1899
Nasjonalgalleriet, Oslo

Plate VII

The sun (sketch). 1912–1913
Munch-Museet, Oslo

74

Plate VIII

Self portrait. Around 1940
Between the clock and the bed.
Munch-Museet, Oslo

83

CHRONOLOGY

Year	Event

1863   Munch was born on December 12th in Loten in the county of Hedmark in Norway. His father was a doctor, his mother frail and gravely ill, family circumstances were greatly reduced. His father was deeply religious, absorbed in his duties to the poor and sick. Norway was an impoverished country, the population for the most part farmers. The educated bourgeois class formed a fast-disappearing minority of the three million inhabitants.

The country was politically linked to Sweden; the years around Munch's birth saw the rise of an increasingly influential movement for Norwegian independence; this, however, was not achieved till 1905.

With their close proximity to Denmark, a few Norwegian artists broke new ground as Romantic painters: Johann Christian Claussen Dahl, who of course established his reputation in Dresden, and Thomas Fearnley, a follower of Constable's. However, the naturalist painter Christian Krohg, who became Munch's teacher, belonged to the subsequent generation of Norwegians.

1864   The Munch family moved to Christiana, as the capital, Oslo, was called till 1924.

1868   Munch's mother died from consumption and tuberculosis. His mother's sister took over the household, brought up the children, and became their much-loved guardian.

At the early age of five young Edvard absorbed into his consciousness his first shattering experience of suffering and death.

1877   Edvard's sister Sophie died at the age of 15, also from tuberculosis.

1879   Edvard Munch took up the study of engineering at the Technical School. Yet as soon as

1880   he took up painting seriously. He left the Technical School and decided to become a painter.

1881   Munch entered Design School and in the same year he succeeded in selling two paintings.

1882   He rented his first studio with six other students, and became a pupil of Christian Krohg.

Krohg was the central painter in the artistic circle in Christiana of the Eighties. He constantly supported Munch, was the first to recognise his ability, and considered him to be the only real talent in the country.

1884   The painter Frits Thaulow, who had good connections with French painters in Paris (he was Gauguin's brother-in-law), was equally firmly convinced of Munch's soaring talents. He bought one of his pictures and also made available a grant to permit him to travel to Paris and study there.

In this year Munch came into close contact with the Bohemian Society, composed of Christiana's avant-garde artists. In the summer he visited Thaulow's open-air academy in Modum.

A legacy provided some financial support.

1885   In May Munch went to Paris for three weeks on the Thaulow grant, went to the Louvre and the Salons, and got to know the work of the Impressionists, in particular Manet.

On his return, he began the masterly paintings of his early period, which were to lead to his breakthrough: "The sick Girl", "The Day After", and "Puberty".

1886   He completed these pictures, and submitted four paintings to the autumn show in Oslo.

1887   He exhibited six pictures, which aroused criticism from his conservative colleagues, the press, and the public.

1888   Munch applied for a state grant, and in

1889   it was granted. His first big exhibition in Christiana, the first one-man show that Norway had ever had, displayed his work to date.

In the autumn, Munch travelled to Paris.

In November, his father died. For Edvard Munch, his death symbolised a break, the end of one period of his life; the outward indication of this was his decision to move to Paris. Artistically, it was reflected in his break with Naturalism, and his move to Symbolism, then just developing into an artistic movement in Paris. On a personal level, his departure from his family meant that he was committed to a restless existence searching for a focal point.

1890   Munch was working at Bonnat's art school in Paris. In May he returned to Norway via Antwerp.

He exhibited 10 paintings at the autumn Salon in Christiana.

His grant was renewed, and he returned to France, but succumbed to rheumatic fever and spent the first two months seriously ill at Le Havre.

Five paintings in store at Christiana were destroyed by fire; Munch received 750 Kroner from the insurance.

1891   After he recovered, Munch travelled to Nice via Paris, returned to Paris in April, and at the end of May went back to Norway via Antwerp. He received a third year's grant from the government, spent the summer in Norway, and went to Paris in the autumn, returning later to Nice. In the autumn he had his first exhibition in Munich.

1892   The years to 1916 were occupied by restless travel; even the winter could not detain Munch in Norway and he went to Nice, returning to Norway in the early spring. In the autumn he received an invitation from Berlin to a big exhibition at the Berlin Artists' Union. The exhibition resulted in uproar, and conservative members forced it to close early. One of the consequences of the controversy was the forming of the Berlin Secession, consisting of advanced factions in Berlin artistic society. A further consequence was that overnight Munch became famous as an artist, in Germany at least.

The exhibition left Berlin and travelled through Germany.

1893   The new year brought many exhibitions: the most important centres were Dresden, Munich, Copenhagen and Berlin, and a large number of paintings were sold.

Munch embarked on a series of pictures: the "Frieze of Life" was taking shape. "Most of my paintings derive from ideas I had in my early youth, more than 30 years ago. But this project preoccupied me so deeply that I never escaped from it, even though I was never asked to complete it by anyone else, nor did anyone who might have been interested in it ever invite me to assemble the whole series of paintings together in one room."

1894   Munch was living and working in Berlin; he spent the summer in Norway and Sweden and the autumn back in Berlin. For several years the city was to be his second home.

Munch had the ability to find inspiration for his work while living in hotel rooms. All through those restless years, much of his output was produced from lonely lodgings, in one hotel after another. The Berlin nights – turbulent and gruelling as they often were – spent for preference among his Norwegian and Swedish friends at the Scandinavian bar called "The Black Pig", which was also frequented by August Strindberg and Stanislaw Przybiyszewski; they were all in love with the latter's lively wife Dagny, whose ebullient vitality was really the hub of this circle, otherwise rather inclined to dourness.

1895   This year too Munch spent at first in Berlin, where he had a large-scale exhibition. In the Paris office the magazine "Pan" sold Munch's etchings, and Julius Meier-Graefe published a Munch portfolio containing eight etchings.

In the summer Munch was at home once more, in the autumn in Paris.

Thadée Naransson published an essay on Munch in the "Revue Blanche" and reproduced the lithograph "The Scream".

1896   The beginning of the year saw Munch back in Paris, where he was gradually acquiring the same recognition as he had in Berlin. He had lithographs and woodcuts printed, and Vollard included the lithographs "Fear" in his "Album des peintres graveurs".

Munch was now concentrating heavily on graphic art, producing a large number of new prints. He contributed to several exhibitions and was working on the illustrations to Charles Baudelaire's "Les Fleurs du Mal"; he had contacts in the theatrical world and designed a stage set. The art dealers Bing and Durand-Ruel displayed an interest in him, and his portraits of Hamsun, Strindberg, and Mallarmé enhanced his reputation in this field, too.

The first studies for "Alpha and Omega" emerged.

1897   Munch was in Brussels for the Symbolist exhibition, where his pictures attracted considerable attention; in June he bought a house in Asgardstrand in Norway.

1898   At first Munch was still in Norway, but in March he travelled via Copenhagen – where he exhibited – to Berlin, and in May on to Paris. But in June he was already back in Norway, where he was to remain till the beginning of the following year.

This period probably marks the beginning of his friendship with Tulla Larsen.

1899   In the spring he embarked on a journey through Berlin to Paris and Nice. From there he continued on to Florence, where he lived at Fiesole, and to Rome. Here, his particular interest was in Raphael, as is evident from his plans for large-scale decorative work.

From June on, Munch was back in Norway: he was forced by illness to spend some time, till the next year, in the Kornhaug Sanatorium.

1902   From the autumn of the previous year, Munch had been in Berlin once more, where he exhibited a sequence of 27 paintings from the "Frieze of Life" in the entrance hall of the Berlin Secession.

Through his friend Albert Kollman, he met Dr. Max Linde in Lübeck, who bought a picture and published a book on Munch. In the summer, the artist was back in Norway. Things were leading up to the quarrel with Tulla Larsen, as a result of which they separated. For a while Munch avoided Norway: his friends had taken Tulla's part and he could not face their reproaches. After a lengthy stay with Dr. Kinde in Lübeck he returned to Berlin, where he struck up an acquaintance with the regional magistrate Gustaf Schiefler, who purchased some prints and started work on the index of the graphic art.

The following year is also marked by successive periods in Paris, Lübeck, and Norway.

1904   Munch's financial situation steadied as a result of his contacts with Bruno Cassirer in Berlin for the sale of prints, and with the Commeter Gallery in Hamburg for paintings. Commeter also undertook to arrange most of his exhibitions for many years.

In this, as in the following year, Munch was constantly involved in restless travel to and fro between Norway, Berlin, and Paris.

1905	Finally, at a big exhibition of Munch's works put on by the Artists' Association in Prague, the "Frieze of Life" was finally shown in its original form.
1906	This year saw the completion of two portraits: one of Harry Graf Kessler and one, done at the instigation of the Stockholm banker Ernest Thiel, the impressive portrait of Friedrich Nietzsche. This is one of the few works Munch did from photographic sources. It is plain from this painting how outstanding was Munch's ability to capture the essential nature of his sitter and to express it in paint.
	In the summer there were theatrical commissions in Berlin which Munch was able to fulfill in 1907.
1907	They took the form of the Reinhardt Frieze, so called after the Berlin director, and were mood paintings for Ibsen's plays.
	The same year in Stockholm, Munch painted the portrait of Ernest Thiel, who bought a large number of pictures.
1908	The first "worker picture" was created. From now on, working men would be an inescapable motif for Munch's paintings. Even in Scandinavia, his outstanding importance was gradually being recognised: Munch was created a knight of the Royal Norwegian Order of St. Olaf.
	Jens Thiijs, the director of the Nasjonagalleriet in Oslo, purchased a number of paintings in spite of violent opposition from conservative factions. A nervous breakdown necessitated another spell in the clinic; contact with his doctor, Dr. Jacobson, improved his psychological condition, and a picture he painted of him acted as a catalyst: "I put him in the picture, tall and big-boned, with all the colours of hell. Then he begged me to spare his life and became as gentle as any dove".
	Munch saw the period he spent in the clinic as a turning-point in his life. He decided to live only for his art: "I felt very brutal when I finally decided to heal myself. I hope this foreshadows a new era for my art".
1909	In May, Munch returned to Norway, where Rasmus Meyer purchased a large number of pictures.
	His prose poem "Alpha and Omega" took shape, with lithographic illustrations; a work that owed its inspiration to Gustav Schiefler. Munch began the sketches for the paintings in the Aula of Christiana. In Norway the largest exhibition of his work to date took place.
1910	The artist needed more space for his work, and acquired the property of Ramme in Hvitsten on Oslo Fjiord in the hope that it would bring improved, less cramped working conditions.
1911	He was finally commissioned to do the designs in the Aula competition. The paintings were to keep him fully occupied till their completion in 1916.

1912 The Separatist Association in Cologne honoured Munch with an exhibition of 32 of his paintings.

   As a result of his stay in Cologne, Munch made the acquaintance of Curt Glaser.

1913 Munch rented the manor of Grimsrod in Jeloya because he needed more room to work.

   His 50th birthday brought a flood of honours. For the first time he was in a position to provide financial support for poverty-stricken young German artists.

1916 Munch bought the estate of Ekely in Skoyen, which was to be the calm centre at the maelstrom of his life. Naturally, it did not become a home in the ordinary sense of the word: the artist was completely uninterested in his personal surroundings, and for a large part of his life he lived in every conceivable kind of lodging, painting under the most difficult circumstances imaginable. We have an account of how Ekely looked at his death: "The artist had lived in this house most modestly, totally dedicated to his work. To the visitor, the interior seemed extraordinary, quite unlike any normal house inhabited by any ordinary mortal. Munch lived in a few sparsely furnished rooms, as though he had never really moved in and were just a chance visitor on his way through – a wandering artist, always on the move ... On the upper storey of the main building, in rooms that had apparently stood empty for years, there were piles of prints ... In one of these box-rooms, Munch had set up his hand press. The room had originally been an old-fashioned kitchen, a gloomy place which had served as a workshop. Everything suggested that Munch attached no importance to cheerfulness at work and did not find it helped his creative enjoyment". (S. Willoch)

   On September 19th., the paintings in the Aula of Christiana University were ceremonially unveiled.

1917 Curt Glaser's book on Munch appeared, and did much to arouse and nurture public interest in Munch's work in Germany.

1922 Edvard Munch received a second large-scale commission: he started work on the murals for the canteen in the Freia chocolate factory in Christiana.

   Munch bought a number of prints from German artists as part of his campaign to support them, a campaign which continued in various forms throughout the ensuing years.

1927 The largest exhibition to date in the Nationalgalerie in Berlin, with 223 oil paintings from all areas of his output was shown.

1929 Munch had his winter studio built in Ekely.

1930	Munch began to suffer from eye trouble, which was to prevent him working the next year and was to reappear several times subsequently.
1933	He was loaded with honours on the occasion of his 70th birthday.
	Jens Thijs and Pola Gauguin published their books on Munch.
1937	A number of Munch's works in German collections were confiscated and declared "degenerate art", along with the works of the other Expressionists.
1940	Munch became seriously ill as a result of the eye trouble that resurfaced in 1938, preventing him from working. At the same time he was much depressed by the political situation.
	He absolutely refused to have any contact with the German invading force or with the Norwegian Quisling régime which was set up under German supremacy. He turned to his work and rejected the outside world.
	Fears that the Nazis might drive him from his house and seize his pictures proved groundless.
	There is no doubt that Munch found the situation easier to bear because he was in the same boat as other outstanding artists, his friends from Germany. Most of his life he had stood alone, outnumbered by his opponents, but now he felt one of a band of fellow-sufferers. Pola Gauguin tells of a visit in 1940, when he found Munch calm and controlled. When Gauguin asked about this unwonted calm, he replied, glancing at the warplanes in the sky: "Do you not understand that all the old ghosts have crept back to their mouseholes for fear of this one great ghost?"
1944	Munch died peacefully in his house in Ekely, wrapped up in his work till his last days. A few days before, he enjoyed the good wishes of friends and admirers on his eightieth birthday, undaunted by the hard times the war had brought.
	In his will, he bequeathed his work to his town, without laying down any conditions as to its disposal.

TABLE OF ILLUSTRATIONS

Where there is no reference to the source of the pictures and prints, they are to be found in the Munch-Museet in Oslo.

The photographic material was kindly made available by the museums, or was in Berghaus' own archives.